The Poetry Of God

The Poetry of God

His Word, His Power, His Presence

Don Baird

The Little Buddha Press
Wake Forest, North Carolina
2021

The Little Buddha Press
710 North Main St.
Wake Forest, North Carolina

The Poetry of God
God's Word — Haiku — Mini-Sermons — Art

Copyright 2021 by Don Baird

Author/Poet: Don Baird
Editor: Don Baird
Cover Design: fiverr
Prayers By: Andrea Sumadsad
Ink Painting by: Don Baird

Bible Passages: "Scripture quotations are taken from the *Holy Bible*, New Living Translation, copyright 1996, 2004, 2015 Tyndale House Foundation. Used by permission of Tyndale House Publishers, Inc., Carol Stream, Illinois 60188. All Rights Reserved.

All rights reserved. No part of this book may be reproduced in any form or by any means, except by a reviewer or scholar who may quote brief passages in a review or article.

Published by The Little Buddha Press
Wake Forest, North Carolina USA
Printed in the United States of America
2021

ISBN #: 978-0-578-98888-7

Acknowledgment

There are many folks that have influenced my life in a thousand wonderful ways. If I name them all, the number of pages in this book will double! In particular, I thank my dearest friends, my wife Maria, and my family for standing by me, helping me, praying for me, and supporting me to lead an effective ministry as well as to remain tenacious enough to complete this unique book.

Preface

God's word contains the finest poetry ever revealed. Within the Bible, His story unfolds with dignity, truth, and love. Through His passion, He gave us His son who became the most incredible shepherd of our Father's living word ever to be born. Jesus remains the greatest teacher of all time. And, according to witnesses, he makes elegant, fine wine.

A humble book, *Poetry of God*, produces an opportunity for readers to enjoy scripture, haiku poetry, and compact sermons. Each page presents God's poetry followed by a haiku and, lastly, a mini-sermon for contemplation. It is my deepest hope that this book encourages readers to ponder God, and to learn more about His word — His desire for us to have happy, joyful, and loving lives, "on Earth as it is with Him."

Please, read *Poetry of God* front-to-back, backwards, bit by bit, and upside down — whatever it takes, make it your pleasure.

(There are, intentionally, no page numbers.)

Let's Pray

Father,

We praise you, we adore you, and we glorify you. We are grateful to you for all that you have done. Thank you that we are all gathered here today to soak in your truth. Your word is our hope. It gives us the will to drive through difficult times.

In moments of darkness,
Father, allow us to realize that all that you have created are for the purpose of good and that what we deal with is not of the flesh and blood alone. Going to battle without you is a lost cause, therefore, we turn to you, Father God. Do give us the tools, clarity, strength, and discernment to settle what we have to in the natural. Matters that are beyond our control and capabilities, we lift them up to you, Lord — for you are greater than them. We surrender not to fear but to faith. Fear reminds us of our limitations while faith reminds us of your unlimited capacity. Enliven love and truth in all of mankind so those who have gone astray may come running back to you.

Father,
Separate and free us from what spoils our lives.

In Jesus' name, we pray.

(all prayers are offered by Andrea Sumadsad)

"Just ask the animals, and they will teach you. Ask the birds of the sky, and they will tell you. Speak to the earth, and it will instruct you. Let the fish in the sea speak to you. [10]For the life of every living thing is in his hand, and the breath of every human being."

Job 12:7-8, 9-10

songbird —
the sound of waves
in a melody

Such a great reminder to keep God as the front runner of your thoughts. The poetic notion that the earth instructs us, that fish speak to us, that birds of the sky are there for us as well, is beyond comprehension! God reaching out; He savors the actions of His people — our wanting to understand — to know more about Him and the habitat that He constructed for us. We cherish God for cherishing us. We long for a relationship with Him as He reaches toward us through every living creature, every planet, each moon, the sound of the ocean, and shooting stars. Reminders of God and His love for us are everywhere! We need to take a moment to realize and enjoy the magnitude of His presence.

"When I look at the night sky and see the work of your fingers— the moon and the stars you set in place — ⁴what are mere mortals that you should think about them, human beings that you should care for them?"

Psalm 8:3-4

peeking through —
moon beams light
the path

God loves us so much. It is incomprehensible how all of this went down. The creator of the Universe thought so highly of us that what He has created, its magnificence, is beyond the grasp of the human mind. I'm amazed just at holding a grain of sand! It's unbelievable how many grains of sand there are on Earth! A shooting star is such a grain; a moon is too; so is the sun; so is the Milky Way; and so is the billion everythings! And then, His final touch — God loves us. Life doesn't get better than this!

"I will be your God throughout your lifetime— until your hair is white with age. I made you, and I will care for you. I will carry you along and save you."

Isaiah 46:4

wrong turn;
in the midst of chaos
His presence

The Bible is fraught with God's promises. This verse contains one of God's most powerful promises — He will be there for us: He will protect, save, and carry us throughout our lives on Earth! I accept the promise! Do you? If you're unsure of what to do, simply tell God, "I'm in." That will do it.

Let's Pray

Father,

Show us what it is like to love like you do. It can be difficult when we have been hurt deeply, wronged or betrayed by those around us, especially if they are people whom we hold dear and trust. Allow us to get over self-centeredness so we can be mindful of others — as what we know about them may barely be scratching the surface of who they really are or what they are going through. They may not know what it feels like to be loved and cared for or they may be too broken as they try to face their own struggles. Grant us greater understanding so we may be slow to anger and judgment. Teach us to let go of frustration and feelings of hate towards our brothers and sisters. Let us be ready to forgive even before it is asked of us or never asked at all, for when we do so, we are not only setting free the people who caused us pain, we unshackle ourselves from the burdens of sorrow, self-pity, and ill thoughts.

In Jesus' name, we pray.

Grace is the free, undeserved goodness and favor of God to mankind
- Matthew Henry

"Let my teaching fall on you like rain;
let my speech settle like dew.
Let my words fall like rain on tender grass,
like gentle showers on young plants."

Deuteronomy 32:2

*light breeze —
the hand of God
on your shoulder*

Our Father is a gentle Father. While He reaches out, He does so in a gentleness that doesn't hurt or offend even the softest of soft people. His "advice and counsel" (His Kingdom) isn't thrown at us but settles on us like dew; His words — a gentle rain. He is sweet; He is beyond kind. Let Him embrace you, let Him show you the Way of Love through His offering of undeserved, unearned Grace. Listen to His heart; learn the secrets of His Kingdom. And then, live by those secrets.

¹"O Lord, you have examined my heart
and know everything about me.

¹⁶Every day of my life was recorded in your book.
Every moment was laid out before a single day had passed.
¹⁷How precious are your thoughts about me, O God. They cannot be numbered!"

Psalm 139:1, 16-17

of all creation;
the lucid thought
of me

God knows everything about us. He has examined each one of us and knows the truth without a filter. No matter what we do or what we think, God is there — right there with us. He guides us without hesitation and loves us whether we are close or far, "Even His hand will guide you." There is no darkness in God. He is the ultimate light, the conquering light that obliterates all darkness — all evil.

"You Light a lamp for me.
The Lord, my God, lights up my darkness."

Psalm 18:28

raising the shades,
my gloom turns to
blessings

There is no darkness for the Lord. All is light, even the dark. He makes it that way. He understands that we often live in darkness — even choose it. So, He lights our way; He illuminates our minds and perceptions in order for us to maintain a wonderful, effective relationship with Him. This is another fantastic example of how God has chosen to serve us. He hopes and anticipates that we will respond likewise.

"But the wisdom from above is first of all pure. It is also peace loving, gentle at all times, and willing to yield to others. It is full of mercy and the fruit of good deeds. It shows no favoritism and is always sincere. ¹⁸And those who are peacemakers will plant seeds of peace and reap a harvest of righteousness."

> James 3:17-18

everlasting —
a shepherd watches over
his sheep

This verse by James, the brother of Jesus, makes it clear that God is the living presence of wisdom — and that His wisdom is pure. God watches us as a good shepherd would to see to it that we are safe, successful, and prosperous. His secrets are an open book to us. We simply need to ask.

Let's Pray

Dear God,

I appreciate that your revelation comes in progression. You unveil more of you unto me, depending on my capacity to accept and receive. You chisel and shape who I become with what happens during my journey with you.

As the path gets steeper and narrower, you broaden my wisdom and understanding to see the traps that the enemy has set before me. When I fall into the cracks, your hand is quick to rescue me.

Having fallen a number of times, I realized that these fissures have one purpose - to separate me from You and from Your love. These crevices may be small and seemingly insignificant in the beginning but they can engulf my entire being once I pay attention to them instead of focusing on you. My hell is separation from you.

In coming to know you, it has been inculcated in me that you will always be bigger than my hell. Your overcoming grace will always be stronger than my suffering.

And so, my Father, I gleefully give my hell to you, that you may freely bring forth your kingdom in me.

In Jesus' name, we pray.

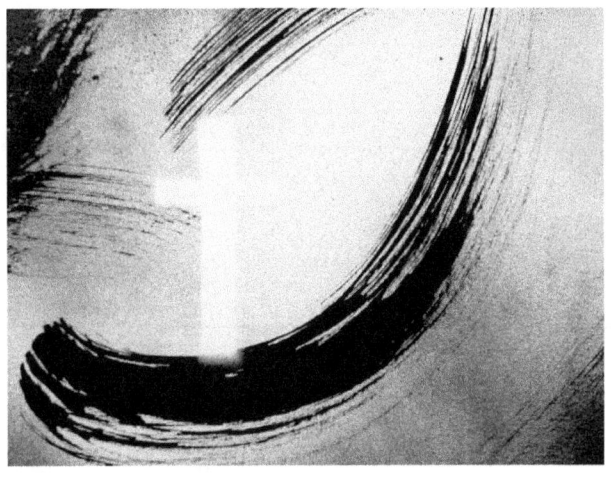

But those who trust in the Lord will find new strength. They will soar high on wings like eagles. They will run and not grow weary. They will walk and not faint."

Isaiah 40:31

> *full moon —*
> *a storm of fear*
> *disappears*

This is an extremely important passage. "But those who trust in the Lord will find new strength." This is saying, exactly, "Those who do not trust the Lord will not find new strength." They will not soar high. They will not be like eagles. They will run and grow weary. And also, "When they walk, they will faint." Isaiah is offering a wakeup call — for the here and now. This isn't something that happens after you're dead. This happens to you, spiritually, right now — without God, there will be a big void in your life — that you will not be the strength, the person, nor the spirit God intended you to be if you are without Him. We have free choice. It is our call. In the end, sure . . . "our bodies return to dust and our spirit returns to God." But there is still a life to live; and to live it with God in your corner, is the best way to go. "For me to live is Christ, and to die is gain." Get rid of ego now. Trust God. Find strength in Him; soar with Him; run with Him without fatigue; and walk at His side for all of eternity!

"Where were you when I laid the foundations of the earth?
Tell me, if you know so much.

5Who determined its dimensions
and stretched out the surveying line?
6What supports its foundations,
and who laid its cornerstone
7as the morning stars sang together
and all the angels[a] shouted for joy?
8"Who kept the sea inside its boundaries
as it burst from the womb,
9and as I clothed it with clouds
and wrapped it in thick darkness?

10For I locked it behind barred gates,
limiting its shores.
11I said, 'This far and no farther will you come.
Here your proud waves must stop!'

12"Have you ever commanded the morning to appear
and caused the dawn to rise in the east?"

Job 38:4-12

*forming clouds . . .
a few sparrows learn
their size*

God has a way of settling things. He is an honest God that lays it out on the table. People can easily access this poem and know themselves. "Tell me if you know so much." Sounds like He is handling a bit of human arrogance? Nothing has changed. Today, millions of people think they're smart enough to handle everything on their own — without even a slight nod to the Creator. Just read the news!!! Oh, where is God right this second? The answer remains, "He is present." He is always present. Are we finally testing His patience? I don't believe so. Remember, He thinks highly of us. He has given us much and continues to do so. And, to our good fortune, He hasn't asked for any of it back! I pray that we can soon live up to His example, His patience, and His grace. The Kingdom of Heaven is on hand. Let's invite the Kingdom of Heaven to be on earth as it is with Him.

"Remember him before the light of the sun, moon, and stars is dim to your old eyes, and rain clouds continually darken your sky. ³Remember him before your legs—the guards of your house—start to tremble; and before your shoulders—the strong men—stoop. Remember him before your teeth—your few remaining servants—stop grinding; and before your eyes—the women looking through the windows—see dimly. ⁴Remember him before the door to life's opportunities is closed and the sound of work fades. Now you rise at the first chirping of the birds, but then all their sounds will grow faint. ⁵Remember him before you become fearful of falling and worry about danger in the streets; before your hair turns white like an almond tree in bloom, and you drag along without energy like a dying grasshopper, and the caperberry no longer inspires sexual desire. Remember him before you near the grave, your everlasting home, when the mourners will weep at your funeral. ⁶Yes, remember your Creator now while you are young, before the silver cord of life snaps and the golden bowl is broken. Don't wait until the water jar is smashed at the spring and the pulley is broken at the well. ⁷For then the dust will return to the earth, and the spirit will return to God who gave it."

Ecclesiastes 12:2-7

hovering your body the last thought of self

Drawn apart, the admonishment is for us to remember Him while we are young. This verse also serves to remind us how much God does for us — how present He is. (I love the word, "present"). God is all good things to us. It's so important for us to remember Him in everything that we do. This is the Way of living a fulfilled life; this is the Way to have heaven on earth. Live this Way now, before you recline to an everlasting grave.

Mourners will weep; but, without God in our lives in every way, we will weep long before we ever pass from this earth. God has personally invited us to have His Kingdom on Earth as it is with Him. We should accept the offer.

Let's Pray

Father,

You are the always and everywhere present God and I am working to be a more present child. I seek that your heart may be found in mine.

Let my faith be reflected in the life I live, not when anyone is looking, but especially in the silent moments between you and me. Contrary to popular belief, allow me to say that you are the farthest thing from typical and boring that has ever been known to me. God, you are the best thing that ever happened — oh, you never happened, you've always been! I was just blind and ignorant to not have noticed sooner. The joy you give me is out this world and is much more potent than Popeye's spinach in a can. I will always be in awe of the never-ending new ways you come up with to express your love for me. If only I can muster a sliver of brilliance to bring forth something that will make you laugh hard on your belly, then I would die smiling.

Father, I pray to be forever smitten in love with you and for the rest of humanity to experience this too.

In Jesus' name, we pray.

"Guard your heart above all else,
        for it determines the course of your life."

Proverbs 4:23

climbing high . . .
a young raccoon falls
into her embrace

This is a very clear admonishment, "Guard your heart . . . above all else . . . it determines the course of your life" — a suggestion for a heart-driven life instead of one defined by intellect. God is not after our minds, our intellect, our I.Q. He is after our hearts, He is after our love, and He is seeking a relationship with us that remains impervious to evil. He asks us to guard our hearts; nothing else. The best way to guard them is to maintain a close relationship with God. I'm in! Are you?

"Don't let anyone think less of you because you are young. Be an example to all believers in what you say, in the way you live, in your love, your faith, and your purity."

1 Timothy 4:12

little lamb —
the sound of Spring
in your heart

Paul advises us to be mature in our relationship with the Kingdom of Heaven, with God. This maturity should be self-evident without regard to our actual age. Every one of us has the ability to be mature in God. In that, it is helpful to watch what we say and how we live — in our love, our faith, and our purity. This is a caring reminder of what we can do here on earth.

"Yet God has made everything beautiful for its own time. He has planted eternity in the human heart, but even so, people cannot see the whole scope of God's work from beginning to end."

Ecclesiastes 3:11

oh moon!
more than the mind
can know

Plain and simple, people cannot see the entirety of God's desire. "From beginning to end" is a thought that can only be fully pondered in the heart — a place where something can be left unsaid but fully known through feeling; the scientific mindset might never be able to complete the task. Yet, the heart is already at peace as it continues to follow God — a path that defies math but embraces the eternal heart — eternal life. What the heart knows is everlasting; what the brain knows is already gone. Love is everlasting; God is everlasting. And, "He has planted eternity in the human heart."

"You light a lamp for me.

The Lord, my God, lights up my darkness."

Psalms 18:28

rising sun . . .
a meadow lark
greets me

This is an important message and, therefore, a recurring commentary (theme) in the Bible. God, Jesus, and the apostles were keen on using this metaphor in their teachings. God lights shadows, darkness in and around us, without hesitation. He is light 24/7. Darkness cannot stand in His presence any more than darkness can stand in front of a working flashlight. Light conquers darkness; darkness does not conquer light. There is no flashlight that emits a dark beam that destroys light. It's a one-way street and God lights the Way.

"And I am convinced that nothing can ever separate us from God's love. Neither death nor life, neither angels nor demons, neither our fears for today nor our worries about tomorrow—not even the powers of hell can separate us from God's love. ³⁹No power in the sky above or in the earth below—indeed, nothing in all creation will ever be able to separate us from the love of God that is revealed in Christ Jesus our Lord."

Romans 8:38-39

ocean waves splash the stars of eternity

Paul was strongly driving this nail home! He was adamant that God's love is permanent. He was convinced that even death could not separate us from God's love — that God's love is everlasting. He was very clear on this idea. This puts a great deal of responsibility on our hearts; we must understand it is true and we should never take advantage of it — and that we never take advantage of God or His Grace.

"For God has not given us a spirit of fear and timidity, but of power, love, and self-discipline."

2 Timothy 1:7

cliff diving;
an ocean pool
of blue

You are created in God's likeness and have the ability to displace fear and timidity. You are God's spiritual DNA of which includes the attributes of power, love, and self-discipline. It is important to keep the Holy Spirit on mind rather than allowing your focus to fixate on things of the Earth. The Spirit of God will keep you strong and vital. Note, when you're feeling fear and timidity, you're not feeling God; you're lost in the things of earth, of humanity. Focus on God and watch your day come alive; watch you come alive!

"This is my command—be strong and courageous! Do not be afraid or discouraged. For the Lord your God is with you wherever you go."

Joshua 1:9

here and there a lion echoes the desert

This verse is pretty cool; and, it is a promise! "God is with you wherever you go." You are never alone. He is at your side at all times. Call on Him. Keep your mind on Him. After all, His promise is letting you know that He is already with you. It is up to you to notice Him, include Him, and to cherish His presence. Don't limit God to being a Sunday School teacher! He is your confidant, your protector, and your courage. It simply takes you to notice.

"So, don't worry about tomorrow, for tomorrow will bring its own worries. Today's trouble is enough for today."

Matthew 6:34

carrying water
the buckets leave
a trail of sweat

Worry is a form of lacking trust. When we worry, we are caught up in ourselves — not focused on God. God is Father. And, like any Father, He loves to give advice and counsel. This fractional commentary of Jesus is huge and meant to remind us to take everything one part at a time — to handle things as they come, and to remain patient. The concept is to keep our minds free from an accumulation of problems, especially ones that haven't arrived yet. Worry is a kind of evil termite: it will chew away at your life, your peace, and your relationship with God. In lieu of worry, pray. Pray constantly.

Let's Pray

We praise you Lord for being our joy. In your presence, we find comfort, peace, and develop strength of faith.

I heard a man say that a seed must first be hidden underneath the earth and break apart before it grows. It does not fulfill its purpose without first going through a series of transitions and transformations.

Father God, we pray to develop steadfast hope and to always delight in you, knowing that even when we feel toppled over by challenges of life, we can trust that you are always working for the good. When we reach our breaking point, you are still moving in us, nourishing our souls just as fertile soil provides sustenance for the seed. The changes may be subtle in the beginning but then it will shoot up from the ground and eventually bear fruit. So too, will we one day bring forth what you have embedded in our hearts, as we grow in your love.

May we always abide in you and celebrate you with unending praise and gladness.

In Jesus' name, we pray.

"He will cover you with his feathers.
He will shelter you with his wings.

His faithful promises are your armor and protection."

Psalm 91:4

temple song;
a voice of strength
calms the storm

The voice of the Holy Spirit calms it all. God's nature is to nurture; it is love; it is mindfulness; it is grace; it is unconditional; it is faithful; it is protective. God, His Holy Essence, is your Father. He covers you with His wings. Know this, absorb the thought, breathe deeply, and be joyful. God is here; God is "at your side."

"Ask me and I will tell you remarkable secrets you do not know about things to come."

Jeremiah 33:3

> *evening prayer —*
> *a promise becomes*
> *new life*

God is all knowing. He is mindful. He made us so that we continue to grow, to discover new and wonderful things that have remained unrevealed for thousands of years. It's all unfolding. In each step of greater understanding, one more step to knowing God is included.

"Love is patient and kind.
Love is not jealous or boastful or proud ^{5}or rude.
It does not demand its own way.
It is not irritable, and it keeps no record of being wronged.
^{6}It does not rejoice about injustice but rejoices whenever the truth wins out.
^{7}Love never gives up, never loses faith, is always hopeful, and endures through every circumstance."

Love will last forever!

1 Cor 13:4-8

purring a cat's tail keeps the tempo

near the fireplace a child's melody

note to note the sound of God's desire

God is describing Himself in this inspirational write of Paul. God is patient and kind. He is truly not jealous (though the culture had a notion at one time that He might be, it isn't so). He has desires but He does not demand. He isn't irritable. He keeps no record of being wronged. How do we know this? Because He is God. Jesus wanted us to know God's perfect nature is absolute Love — ceaseless and unwavering.

"The Lord is my shepherd;
I have all that I need.
²He lets me rest in green meadows;
he leads me beside peaceful streams.
³He renews my strength.
He guides me along right paths,
bringing honor to his name."

Psalm 23:1-4

*quenching thirst . . .
sheep rest in the silence
of themselves*

Oh, the peace this makes me feel. Such an amazing poem. What a rich presentation of God as our Shepherd and of His love that He has for us. "I shall not want," is a phrase about having everything that you need — all of it. Of course, this is a spiritual reference; but think about it further — the Earth has been supplying humanity's needs since their creation! Amazing! And now, through Jesus we have been renewed — we have been renewed through His grace. We can absolutely rest in the green meadows of our hearts. We can clearly drink the pure and calm water of God's wisdom. And we can cherish the thought that God cherishes us!

Let's Pray

*Father,
we celebrate your Presence, for in your presence is fullness of joy. You said "I Am", as you are always in the moment. We are sure to find you when we seek with all our hearts. Place within us your Holy Spirit so we are always motivated and filled with perseverance to show up and participate with you. Fix our focus so we can appreciate and savor our relationship. May we not be preoccupied by looking at how you are working on our neighbors' lives that we miss what you are doing in our own.*

*Father,
help us accept what we cannot change but only heal and learn from and remove the worries we get by looking so far ahead that we forget we need to concentrate on the now in order to get there. What we choose as the origin of our joy determines how long it would last. If we put our joy into our own youth, we'd start turning into sad prunes the minute the first grey hair shows up. If we put gladness into having possessions then it's sure to run out. You are the only source that doesn't need a gauge because your rivers are certain to flow and never dry up.*

The fullness of joy is in your presence. May we take this to heart and never forget.

In Jesus' name, we pray.

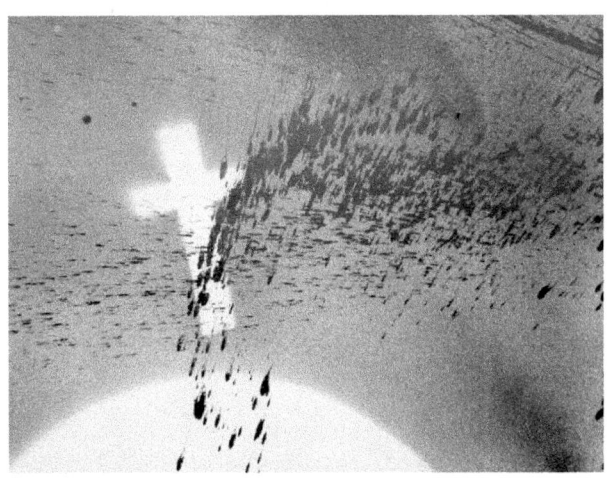

"But those who trust in the Lord will find new strength.
They will soar high on wings like eagles."

Isaiah 40:31

hovering a commanding voice opens the way

Trust is often a difficult attribute to acquire. It is illusive, hard to define, and harder to live by. God is love; God is also trust: He has never let us down — we do that ourselves. We can slow this process of letting ourselves down by strengthening our relationship with God. His Holy Spirit, His Holy Nature hovered the waters; it doesn't end their though — He hovers us as well! We simply need to open our hearts and continue to ask Him in, to continue being conscious of Him, and His presence. His Spirit hovers us all day, all night, and forever — God is never not present. Find your strength in Him. He is unwavering in His desire to help us soar.

"Come to me, all of you who are weary and carry heavy burdens, and I will give you rest."

Matthew 11:28

small talk
the familiar words
of wine

When things become too overwhelming, give it to God. He is the answer even when you might not think so. Don't doubt. Have faith and confidence that He is interested in you and that He constantly reaches out to you, not just to help you carry your burdens, but to completely take them away.

"And be sure of this: I am with you always, even to the end of the age."

Matthew 28:20b

rainbow from one end to the other

God will never leave us, never abandon us. He is in this for the long haul. We are not accidents of nature; we are a result of His intention. Think on that; pray on that; and, never forget that.

Let's Pray

*Thank you, Lord,
that nothing happens by accident. You govern the direction of the winds. The ocean's raging waters become still at your command. You have everything under control and all you allow is driven with divine reason that isn't necessarily revealed at once. Father, please open our eyes so we become aware of where you stand in our current situation, instead of us realizing your presence only in hindsight. May we never tire of choosing to trust you, especially at temptation's door. As we develop a deeper connection with you, may we take to heart that you define who we are, so we need not be restricted to measures of mere men. Lord, in having this partnership with you, bless us with discernment to know where our part ends so that you can begin and take over. Let us not be hindered by our own arrogance and egoistic nature. Guide us in living lives that are in accordance to your
will and not against your purposes.*

In Jesus' name, we pray.

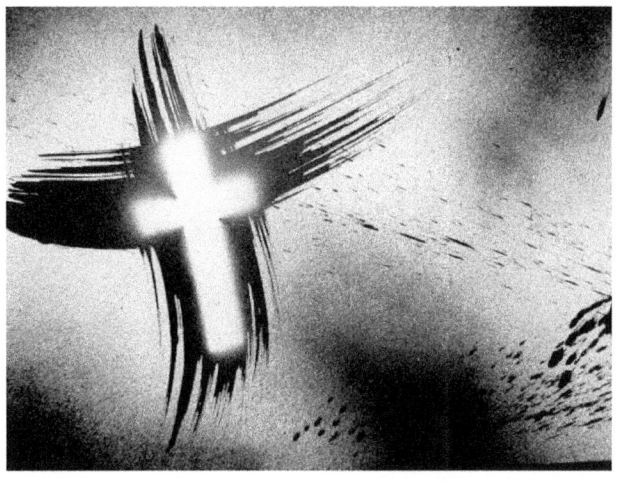

"Many people say, "Who will show us better times?"
Let your face smile on us, Lord.

⁷You have given me greater joy
than those who have abundant harvests of grain and new wine.

⁸In peace I will lie down and sleep,
for you alone, O Lord, will keep me safe."

Psalm 4:6-8

shooting star
is that your smile
near the moon?

What a comfort!!! What a joy in knowing our Creator, our God, our Father! He has given us such abundance; He has served us as a servant and yet He is our one, our only, steadfast God — the true Father of All things! There is nothing that He did not create. And, everything that He did create, He did so for us. He loves us. He serves us peace whenever we reach out to Him. We should reach out to Him often. "In peace, I will lie down and sleep."

"My enemies, whom I have never harmed,
hunted me down like a bird.

⁵³They threw me into a pit
and dropped stones on me.

⁵⁴The water rose over my head,
and I cried out, "This is the end!"

⁵⁵But I called on your name, Lord,
from deep within the pit.

⁵⁶You heard me when I cried, "Listen to my pleading!
Hear my cry for help!"

⁵⁷Yes, you came when I called;
you told me, "Do not fear."

Lamentations 3:52-57

*coyote tracks;
the sound of thunder
clears the air*

Sometimes we find ourselves in situations that are so evil that it's difficult to comprehend. However, whatever it is that we cannot understand, God does. When He says, "Do not fear," He isn't kidding. Keep your relationship with God active. You will find that He is a living verb of action. Keep faith.

"Lord, you have heard the vile names they call me.
You know all about the plans they have made.
^{62}My enemies whisper and mutter
as they plot against me all day long.
^{63}Look at them! Whether they sit or stand,
I am the object of their mocking songs."

Lamentations 3:61-63

ocean waves . . .
consuming the sand
under their feet

People from all ages have reached out to God for help. Every one of us has run across difficult, evil people. They do, indeed, call names, whisper, and mutter; they sneak around in their nasty little way to drum up hurtful things to do to people. They live in the shadows of empty hearts and misery. However, God is a triumphant God and He will serve and protect His sheep. He will pull the foundation of these culprits right out from under their feet and place them under Christ's footstool! He loves you! Call on Him any time — and always.

Let's Pray

*Awaken me, my first love.
Give me the grace to not shy away from you but instead to press in all the more. Trample away iniquity and deceit from my sphere of influence and let me see with your vision that I may not be blind as to where evil has worked to perverse and infiltrate the purity of life. Peel off the layers of my external worldly armor and install in me your living word. Your protection is all the protection I need. Light me up with the fire of your love and let me pass on a spark to every being that I come across with or touch. Enable your healing presence to flow in me and through me to wipe away discord. Father, thank you for allowing me to partner with you, for your will to be done on earth as it is in Heaven. I celebrate your glory.*

In Jesus' name, I pray.

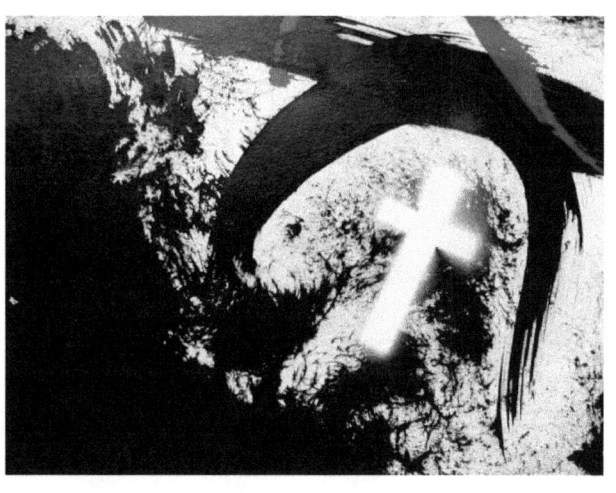

"But let all who take refuge in you rejoice;
let them sing joyful praises forever.

Spread your protection over them,
that all who love your name may be filled with joy.

¹²For you bless the godly, O Lord;
you surround them with your shield of love."

    Psalm 5:11-12

> *Milky Way —*
> *the everywhere of*
> *your reach*

There is nowhere that is out of reach for God, our Father. His arms are the length of love — never ending. His thoughts about us are high, so much so that He gave us dominion over the earth and all its things! Who are we that He would think so well of us? Within His reach, within His grasp, He and He alone is our shield of love.

"O Lord, hear me as I pray;
   pay attention to my groaning.

²Listen to my cry for help, my King and my God,
   for I pray to no one but you.

³Listen to my voice in the morning, Lord.
   Each morning I bring my requests to you and wait expectantly."

   Psalm 5:1-3

breaking silence,
the voice of a dove
answers your call

I imagine that most folks have had, in at least one occasion, the question, "Is God really listening to me, is He going to respond?" David was praying to God, begging for Him to listen and yet, he, without a doubt, knew in his heart that he could and should wait "expectantly." Through his lifetime of experiences with God, he knew that God would absolutely answer his prayers. When you pray, when you commune with God, be sure to be patient — but, expectantly. God will respond, He will answer in His own Way and in His own time. He knows the larger picture; you know the smaller picture: let God do what He does best — everything!

"Above this surface was something that looked like a throne made of blue lapis lazuli. And on this throne high above was a figure whose appearance resembled a man. [27]From what appeared to be his waist up, he looked like gleaming amber, flickering like a fire. And from his waist down, he looked like a burning flame, shining with splendor. [28]All around him was a glowing halo, like a rainbow shining in the clouds on a rainy day. This is what the glory of the Lord looked like to me. When I saw it, I fell face down on the ground, and I heard someone's voice speaking to me."

Ezekiel 1:26-28

*rainbow —
a glimmer of God
reveals His glory*

We should "fall to the ground" daily. God's wisdom is difficult to hear until we become completely humbled. It is impossible to have the Kingdom of God "on Earth as it is with Him" until we become a rich soil that His guidance can abide in. When He abides in us, we can abide in Him. Humbleness is the door to mutuality with our Father. Fall to the ground (physically or metaphorically). Offer yourself to God without hesitation today. Become soil, become earth, become ready for God to plant His wisdom, His counsel, His advice. Know God by opening the door — and the only door that gives God complete access to us is the door of humbleness. In other words, make yourself less, then God will become more. When He becomes more in you — in your heart, He will lift you up and you too will become more! The paradox: if you want to become more, to God, you must first become less to yourself.

"Joy has left our hearts; our dancing has turned to mourning.

¹⁶The garlands have fallen from our heads.
Weep for us because we have sinned.

¹⁷Our hearts are sick and weary,
and our eyes grow dim with tears.

¹⁹But Lord, you remain the same forever!
Your throne continues from generation to generation.

²¹Restore us, O Lord, and bring us back to you again!
Give us back the joys we once had!"

Lamentations 5:15-17, 19, 20-21

*mourning,
clouds become
our restoration*

The one and only reason we will ever experience lost hope is when we have lost our active relationship with God. When our lives become too clouded (through mind, through tears) we become incapable of having a good relationship with God. The feeling of "joy and dancing in our hearts" will be impossible to retain when we are separate from God. There is an illusion that can set in, though, giving us the falsehood that, "We are just fine without God", but there isn't any truth to it. Love begins and ends with God; it is His nature, His gift. There are no shortcuts. When we feel otherwise, we are not living truth, we are a living falsehood, a falsehood that can easily lead to destruction right here and right now — on earth. Joy will return when God returns — "Ask and you shall receive." This is a powerful reference to God's Holy Spirit, His very Nature. Ask God, His Holy Spirit to dwell in your heart. Become His once again. When you do, you will no longer be sick and weary; you will be restored in Him, forever! Let His grace and wisdom guide your life. You'll live the difference.

Let's Pray

*Father,
we all have a unique story and where we are on our walk with you have varying points. Teach me to not bring judgement upon my neighbors when I perceive that there is something that does not add up in their relationship with you. It is not my position to judge anyway. Do not let me forget that I was once in their shoes, and probably further away from where they are standing in proximity to you. Let me be supportive of their turning points. We come to you for different reasons during different seasons. Although our intentions are not always correct and just, you always have what we need anyway. Instead of grumbling about what should and shouldn't be, I just praise you for who you are. Because I know, that once my heart opens from you doing what only you can do, restoration happens, and transformation comes forth.*

I trust the Maker knows what needs fixing and how to fix it.

In Jesus' name, we pray.

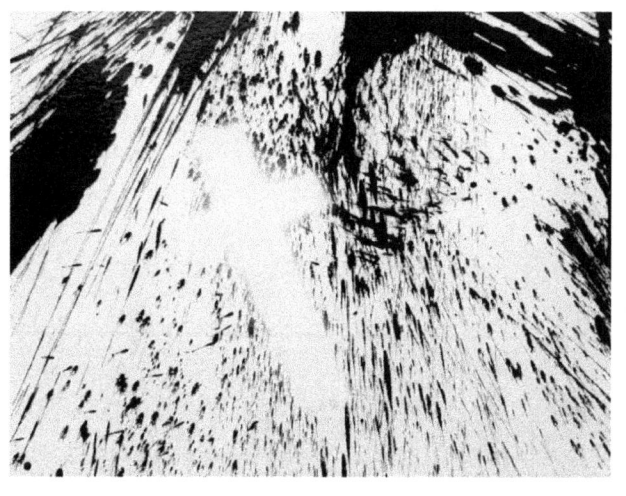

"The voice said to me, "Son of man, eat what I am giving you—eat this scroll! Then go and give its message to the people of Israel." ²So I opened my mouth, and he fed me the scroll. ³"Fill your stomach with this," he said. And when I ate it, it tasted as sweet as honey in my mouth."

Ezekiel 3:1-2

banquet;
the love of God is
our nourishment

"Son of man" is an Aramaic phrase meaning "human being." This verse is filled with descriptive, metaphorical language (very common in Jewish custom). Open your heart to God. He will "feed you His scroll" is a poetic way of saying, "Become humble and then I can reach you." This is a major theme of the Bible of which indicates what the culture had become. It also denotes that God is still reaching out, that God is endeavoring to return our attention back to Him so that He can guide us and serve us His wisdom. A chef cannot feed a closed mouth. Yes, He can create stunning food but it remains on us to eat it! God's lessons are "sweet as honey." But our hearts, when closed with arrogance, will never accept even the "sweetest of foods." Our Father has honey for us! Why do we sit around with our mouths closed — our ears closed, our hearts closed when He, Himself, is desiring to serve us? God wants to serve us! Can you imagine?

"As I looked, I saw a great storm coming from the north, driving before it a huge cloud that flashed with lightning and shone with brilliant light. There was fire inside the cloud, and in the middle of the fire glowed something like gleaming amber."

Ezekiel 1:4

glowing —
a sudden thunder reveals
His Glory

The Holy Spirit is fire, presence, and power — the very nature of God. Take your dark glasses off and become overwhelmed with His light. Let the Holy Spirit guide your every action; let Him abide in you in everything that you do. Ask your Father to become the thundering storm of your life! His storm is one that builds rather than destroys; it is one of renewal and unceasing hope.

Jesus prays, 'Father, if you are willing, remove this cup from me. Nevertheless, not my will but yours be done."

Luke 22:42

torrential wind;
an oak bends in the
presence of God

Prayer is something to respect. God, our Father is someone to respect, even adore. When Jesus prayed this prayer, it was substantially the most crucial prayer ever to be prayed. He, in a significant moment, prayed for God's will to be done, not his own. Of anything he could have requested, he wanted only to please his Father. This stands out as an exemplary moment of prayer. When we pray, what do we pray for? Do we pray for our own will to be done; do we acquiesce to the desires of our Father? God knows what we want before we ask. And yet, we ask for everything under the sun. Jesus is our oak. He bends before the Father, to his Father's desire rather than to his own. Jesus died on the cross. Next time you have a challenge, next time you offer a prayer to God, understand that God's answer comes from wisdom we can't imagine. All prayers are answered; but they are not answered from our wisdom — they are answered from our Father's.

Let's Pray

*Thank you, Father God
for bringing us together today to commune with you, to constantly learn from
each other and broaden our understanding of you along the way. Lord, we pray that you minister to us so that we live to take action on the milk of your word. In pointing our focus on you, may we know who we truly are. May we reflect your nature at all times — and as still waters mirror the beauty of an impeccable sky, we wish to point others in your direction so they may also discover
who they are in Christ.*

In Jesus' name, we pray.

"And this is the confidence that we have toward Him, that if we ask anything <u>according to His will</u>, He hears us."

    1st John 5:14-15

all-the-day,
a soaring hawk
beckons truth

"If we ask anything according to His will, He hears us." What if we ask something that is not of His desire? It sounds like He will tune us out leaving us to ourselves. We are taught in this lesson to seek God's will and not our own. In the prayer that Jesus offered before his crucifixion, he relinquished his will to that of his Father. How should we pray, then? Do we ask according to our will or according to the desire of God? Jesus says to pray in his name. "In my name" is an Aramaic idiom for "in my way." This means, copy me. "In Jesus's way, I pray ......"Well, how did he pray? He prayed in the overarching framework of, "According to His (God's) will/desire." Our job is to copy the ethic that Jesus keenly presented through his personal actions.

"Pray without ceasing."

1 Thessalonians 5:17

ever-present
the pines, the moon, the stars
ever present

This is a suggestion to keep our minds and our communication on God at all times. No matter what, we remember that God is present, we have a relationship with Him, and regardless of our choices in life, we should include Him without ceasing. We do not always have to be asking Him for something. We absolutely can relate to Him throughout the day, bringing Him close. Going to church is not a relationship with God; abiding in God 24/7 is.

> "Our Father in Heaven
> may your name be kept holy"
>
> Matthew 6:9

shooting star . . .
your unique journey
just for us

Awoon is an Aramaic word for father, referencing a personal, family relationship. Jesus used this word to reveal that our God, our Father should be treated in an endearing manner. He is saying, "Our Awoon," to mix languages for a moment. Dwashmaya means heaven, universal, universe, everywhere (and beyond). In this instruction on how to pray, He uses the word to indicate that God, (our Father) is everywhere, without exception. Holy, as translated from Aramaic, means to be set aside (for something very special) and never used out of that context — perfect specialness. God is that special. His name was never mentioned; He was only referenced. Why would we set His name aside? What is the purpose? It's simple, actually. God's name was to be never used — it was too special — He is too special. God should be set aside for a single purpose — to commune with. We now have the following for an interesting translation of Jesus's teaching:

our Father who is everywhere (present)
we set your name aside for communing

From time to time, people make God too cheap. Through sincere studies of Aramaic culture, idioms, metaphors, and their typical style of storytelling, we can become much closer to our Father, as God, as family; through our studies, we can become closer to God — more respectful of Him, without reservation.

"The sinful nature wants to do evil, which is the opposite of what the Spirit wants. And the Spirit gives us desires that are the opposite of what the sinful nature desires. These two forces are constantly fighting each other, so you are not able to carry out your good intentions."

Galatians 5:17

borrowing . . .
how many pens
do you have?

This is such an interesting write of Paul. He was continuously wrestling with himself. He recognized the desire of the Holy Spirit of God; he wanted the Spirit to be completely active in his life, without distraction. It was a challenge for him every single moment he was alive. He fought against his sinful nature with all his might. He realized that these two forces were not going anywhere soon, that this is life's matrix and he had to, as we all do, learn how to handle it. He was committed to God, to Jesus. There was no turning back. In a way, we are following Paul's footsteps even if we don't choose to. This is the situation of human life. Accept it, live it, pray about it, stay close to our Father, and move forward. Take God into your heart; accept His grace through your Faith. Do your very best. And, live!!! Remember, Paul said, "So I live in this earthly body by trusting in the Son of God who loved me and gave himself for me," *Galatians 2:20b*.

Let's Pray

Father,

We offer you thanks and praise. We are grateful to be gathered here today to learn and grow in you. We desire to be reformed in Christ, our Savior. Father, we pray for our faith to be invulnerable so it cannot be smeared by the vileness that surrounds us. Please do not let other people's fear poison our courage. Also, Father, let not what is ignoble in us spoil what is good in others. Lead us to build each other up rather than letting us tear one another down. Guide us to be generous in acts of love, as you are boundless in giving mercy and grace.

In Jesus' Name, we pray.

"But God is so rich in mercy, and He loved us so much, ⁵that even though we were dead because of our sins, He gave us life when He raised Christ from the dead. **It is only by God's grace that you have been saved!**"

Ephesians 2:4-5

*convicted —
dying with Christ
to live again*

Paul makes a distinction, throughout his writings, that grace comes from God while faith comes from Jesus. Through our faith we live a better life on earth (as it is in heaven). This is our goal; this was Jesus's goal; this was God's goal. Grace is forever; faith is for here and now — faith, is an operative word that leads us to our personal "forevers." We have been given Grace — an eternal life in heaven with God, our Father. We have also been given the opportunity to have the "Kingdom of Heaven on Earth." It is our choice. We die with Christ (our egos completely annihilated) to be reborn — to be complete through the actions and teachings of Jesus. May we all keep forming in Jesus's Way; may we all be complete in God and Him in us.

"But the fruit of the Spirit is love, joy, peace, patience, kindness, goodness, faithfulness, gentleness, and self-control."

Galatians 5:22

wood peckers awaken the forest

    rising sun still rising

        snagged by wire a lamb set free

            savoring again the moon's fullness

                holding back I follow the Way

The Holy Spirit is God's very nature. It is impossible for us to list all of the attributes of the Holy Spirit. However, Paul has revealed a few key ones that we can begin to model ourselves after. As we become these through our studies, actions, and prayer, we will discover more about God and continue to mature in His presence. It seems simple yet humanity persists in a sort of non-consensus where separation and dissonance remain pervasive — often invasive. What can we do? Where do we start? We must keep praying, we must keep forming in Christ. When we resign ourselves, we will gain ourselves. This is a recurring theme of the Bible and of our relationship with God, our Father. When we make God first, He will lift us up — higher than we ever dreamed.

Let's Pray

*We invite your presence, Father.
Let your Holy Spirit be upon us, and in us, as we gather today in your name
to give you praise and gratitude.*

Lord, we thank you that we are all here, safe and in abundance of your mercy and love. We thank you, for you love us so fervently — that you sent your son to carry all our pains, infirmity and suffering. We place all of our own burdens at the foot of his cross and receive the blessing that comes with his resurrection — that we are recreated and made whole again. With open arms, we receive the great plans you have in store for us. We acknowledge that you bring life and healing so that we can carry peace in our hearts. Bless us, Father, that as we receive your love and forgiveness, we may also be quick to forgive those who have offended us, that we may choose to be kind and loving even in difficult moments. Make our faith firm that we may stand strong in the face of an adversary. Restore sympathy and empathy that have died in us so we may be sensitive to the needs and cries of our neighbors and not think twice about extending a helping hand. Bring us in unison that we may all be instruments of your goodness and so we may bring glory back to you, as it should be.

In Jesus' name, we pray.

"And this is the way to have eternal life — to know you, the only true God, and Jesus Christ, the one you sent to earth."

    John 17:3

weaving stars
thoughts of God
resurrected.

We continue to search for truth. We hope to find "more to this life" than what we have. Without true meaning, what is it all for? We are born; we die: that's it? Ponder the stars. Go outside, be still, and look. Zillions of miles are right before your eyes — that alone should help you feel and know God, our Father, our Creator. He bestowed upon us the greatest experience we could possibly have — life and love. And, it is Him who loved us first and sent us the greatest messenger of love to reach out to us — Jesus Christ. Jesus was and is our mediator, our priest, our prophet, and our spiritual king. He taught us that our Father is everything, that our Father is everything powerful. He taught us to offer our entire soul to him. He is God, our Beloved; He is the single source of life.

"I pray that they will all be one, just as you and I are one — as you are in me, Father, and I am in you. ²³May they experience such perfect unity that the world will know that you sent me and that you love them as much as you love me."

John 17:21, 23

for our pleasure —
the moon, the sun
become one

> *full eclipse;*
> *our desires bow*
> *in His presence*

abiding . . .
billions of fish
swim the sea

God's steadfast goal is to bring us to Him, fully and completely. He wants us to be aligned with Him as He is aligned with us. Jesus and God are aligned — perfectly. Jesus died on the cross as they had planned — to impact us with the importance of absolute alignment and to denote to us that we must have faith and that we must persevere in that faith. God, Jesus and us, should abide in each other — a "one for all and all for one" spiritual relationship that is eternal. That is their purpose; is it ours? When it is our desire too, we will fully abide — fully align with them both and enjoy the Kingdom of Heaven here on earth. They have chosen; we can choose — and, we should.

"I thank God that I speak in languages more than any of you. ¹⁹But, in a church meeting, I would rather speak five understandable words to help others than ten thousand words in an unknown language."

1 Corinthians 14:18-19

> *crying out*
> *a lion announces*
> *his way*

Often, arguments about the "this and that" of God occur — the theology of God. As intellects surface, hearts submerge into an abyss. "You will seek me and find me when you seek me with all your heart," ~ *Jeremiah 29:13*. This cannot be any clearer — it isn't intellect, it isn't words that attract people to God; it is heart. Words are words, but the heart is the house of love, the house of God within. Speak the language of love and everyone can understand. Love is the one and only universal language without regard to race, creed, or beliefs. Unspoken love is the best argument for God. In silence, in few words, follow His Way — invite God's Kingdom of Heaven to be on earth as it is with Him.

Let's Pray

Father,
we start this prayer with Praise and Thanksgiving. We thank you for being in control over our lives and, as such, we need not ever worry. We trust that you meet our every need, even the ones that have not yet come to the Light of our awareness. We thank you Lord for the people who have prayed for us in our times of bewilderment, wandering, and trouble. In the same Way you have sent them to pray for us; so, we pray for our brothers and sisters.

Father we ask that you reveal yourself to each of them in the way they need to see, hear, feel, and experience you. Send forth your son, Jesus into their Hearts to still the waves of turmoil from within. May they find the clarity and peace they are seeking in Christ. Heal them where they need to be healed, Father. Ignite in them the thirst to seek you above all else. Fill and consume them with your Holy Spirit, Lord, so they may heed and abide in its guidance. Grant them not only enough faith to begin their walk with you, but also for the fortitude to finish the journey. May the Holy Spirit solidify their relationship with you and, in that, may their deepest, darkest wounds be healed.

We praise and celebrate how you are actively transforming us in every way that only you can imagine.

In Jesus' Name, we pray.

"**Delight yourself in the Lord**, and He will give you the desires of your heart."

Psalm 37:4

purring
near the window, a cat
watches the sunrise

Something so simple isn't simple at all — the sunrise, a cat purring. Can you imagine being God who invented it, "I know, I will make the universe so beautiful for people, I will include wonderous things called "sunrise," and "sunset." People will be in awe and write music, poetry, and dream of their futures while they simply observe one of these two gifts." What a glorious God that we have! What an incredible shepherd that we have — what an amazing Creator that we have!!! He gave us everything for our joy, our hearts, our passion, and beyond. God is beyond words; He is fully heart, and yet, gloriously mindful. It's time for us to take a few moments and emulate the cat purring by the window, giving glory to God for all that He has created just for us. And, it's probably a really appropriate thing to do when we say, "I'm sorry Father, I have intended to be more loving, more grateful, and more concerned with your creation than I have been. God, you have made us all caretakers. You have made us so that we have the ability to work together; yet, we often (most often) choose not to." Well, it's time for us to step up, join in as a team of folks who trust their lives to God and to become good shepherds that delight in His presence as they watch over His creation.

"The Lord is not slow to fulfill His promise as some count slowness, but is patient toward you, not wishing that any should perish, but that all should reach repentance."

2 Peter 3:9

fishing
an old man
reaches out

"Perish" is a translation of an Aramaic word that has many possibilities for translation. The Jews were saying, in their way, that people are cast aside, kind of banished if they did not repent (turn back to God). Western civilization would claim they perish, suffer complete ruin, or destruction. But perish in that sense is not a Jewish concept. The word has been taken out of cultural context to mean something the Jews wouldn't know about or believe in. This word, perish, in Aramaic means something closer to *banished, left aside, separated,* even *ignored.* It's like, there is a party and the people who have turned away from God will not be there. It's not a direct punishment as people would have you believe. It's more like, "Leave the house. Come back when you're ready to take the glory you have for yourself and give it to God. In the meantime, you're on your own.

"For I am the least of all the apostles. In fact, I'm not even worthy to be called an apostle after the way I persecuted God's church."

1 Corinthians 15:9

wind storm
the way the snail rolls
into safety

We, from time to time, could think of ourselves as unworthy. We might feel the "less than" that we are because, well, we just aren't perfect. It's the way things are. And, you know, God made us that way. We were made to feel and experience the "good and bad" of things; we were created to dwell in the matrix of free choice; we were made to experience and feel our choices, whether good or bad. This matrix allows us the ability to experience life in its fullest extent. Love/hate, good/bad, ecstasy/pain, peace/unrest, joy/sadness are only a few of the unlimited pairings that we will experience. Paul was caught in guilt through his actions of persecuting the church. He understood his vision with Jesus while at the same time, thought himself to be unworthy of such a journey. He suffered greatly. But it is true that God selected him to carry Jesus's message to the gentiles. And, you know, he did an amazing job and he stood as an example of the power of God's grace. Paul remained committed to God, to Jesus, and to his mission. We are all a little bit like Paul — we fail in some way, we fall short. And we, like Paul, have been chosen; we have been given "grace through faith." It is God's gift — His award — and there is "nothing that we can do to earn it." Through God's indescribable wisdom, we are without exception, offered His undeserved grace. We are blessed by Him, personally; we should be humble, accept His gift, and know that our Father, without reservation, considers us worthy.

"The faithful love of the Lord never ends!

His mercies never cease.
²³ Great is his faithfulness;
his mercies begin afresh each morning.
²⁴ I say to myself, "The Lord is my inheritance;
therefore, I will hope in him!"
²⁵ The Lord is good to those who depend on him,
to those who search for him.
²⁶ So it is good to wait quietly
for salvation from the Lord.

²⁹ Let them lie face down in the dust,
for there may be hope at last.

³¹ *For no one is abandoned
by the Lord forever."*

Lamentations 3:22-26, 29, 31
(Ezekiel)

*lamenting . . .
he embraces the cup
he must drink from*

When you read the first line followed by the last one, the overarching message of the Bible comes together flawlessly. God's message is absolute; it rings like a church bell throughout the city — throughout your personal, guttural "knowing." The question is, "Do we hear the bell or not?" The next question is, "Do we listen to its message?" This bell is a prophetic bell that rings throughout the hearts of humanity. "For, no one is abandoned by the Lord forever." We are all under His grace — for eternity.

"There are also bodies in the heavens and bodies on the earth. The glory (beauty, delight) of the heavenly bodies is different from the glory of the earthly bodies. [41] The sun has one kind of glory, while the moon and stars each have another kind. And even the stars differ from each other in their glory.
[42] It is the same way with the resurrection of the dead. Our earthly bodies are planted in the ground when we die, but they will be raised to live forever. [43] Our bodies are buried in brokenness, but they will be raised in glory. They are buried in weakness, but they will be raised in strength. [44] <u>They are buried as natural human bodies, but they will be raised as spiritual bodies. For just as there are natural bodies, there are also spiritual bodies.</u>

[50] What I am saying, dear brothers and sisters, is that our physical bodies cannot inherit the Kingdom of God. These dying (mortal) bodies cannot inherit what will last forever.

[51] But let me reveal to you a wonderful secret. We will not all die, but <u>we will all be transformed</u>! [52] It will happen in a moment, in the blink of an eye, when the last trumpet is blown. For when the trumpet sounds, those who have died will be raised to live forever. And we who are living will also be transformed. [53] For our dying (mortal) bodies must be transformed into bodies that will never die; our mortal bodies must be transformed into immortal bodies."

1 Corinthians 15:40-42, 50-53

oh caterpillar
how did you become
a butterfly?

People often get confused about what's going to happen when they die. Paul touches on it in this passage, "What I am saying . . . is that our physical bodies cannot inherit the Kingdom of God." He continues by sharing with us that we will be transformed (all of us). We will transform into new selves in bodies that will be eternal.

In a way, we will have "new clothing" just as the caterpillar does — the butterfly being beautiful. In one life, she is a caterpillar; in the next, she is a butterfly; lastly, she is spirit — another new body? This is all such a mystery to us. Jesus taught us so much about living, how to do it well. He taught us a lot about his own death to come. However, much mystery remains as to what happens to us. One thing we are told in very clear words, "Dust returns to the earth, the spirit returns to God," ~ *Ecclesiastes 12:7*. Our bodies are the dust. There is nothing we can do to change it. It is God's immaculate design.

Let's Pray

Lord, everyone has a fatal flaw but you are far greater than each one's hamartia. We thank you, Father for your boundless grace and mercy. Open our hearts and minds, Father God, to heal our skewed desires and flawed perceptions. Help us come to a better understanding that perseverance and passion of a wrong thing does not make it right. Drive us to outgrow the bad habit of overlaying our own preferences and prejudices on a concept, warping it into something that will fit our personal ideals rather than yours. May our ideas not become our idols, but purify our dreams so we may serve your purpose instead of the immature whims of our hearts and flesh. May your Holy Spirit guide us in discerning the difference between fantasy and Truth. Cleanse our desires, Lord, that we may delight in wanting the things that are of you. May we have absolute faith in you; may we know through our faith, that your bountiful love will never steer us in the wrong direction.

In Jesus' name, we pray.

"Though I am surrounded by troubles,
   you will protect me from the anger of my enemies.
You reach out your hand,
   and the power of your right hand saves me."

Psalm 138: 7

torrential downpour a sudden calm interrupts

In the midst of an insurmountable attack, God's hand touches you with His glory — His power. In awe, evil the coward, withdraws; it runs to protect itself. Peace comes over you as the Lord stands at your side. When He puts His hand on you, you're saved. It's that simple. When you have a relationship with God, you are in good hands. He is with you at all times, in everything you do. This doesn't mean that He gives you all that you ask for. He is a discerning Father and is always working for the greater good of humanity. It's imperative to have faith in Him. Leave your storms with Him; give all burden to Him. "So do not fear, for I am with you; do not be dismayed, for I am your God. I will strengthen you and help you; I will uphold you with my righteous right hand, ~ *(Isaiah 41:10)*.

"Dear brothers and sisters, when troubles of any kind come your way, consider it an opportunity for great joy!"

James 1:2

> *sunrise . . . sunset*
> *sweat waters the first*
> *seedlings*

Our challenges bring us closer to God. He is our wisdom, He is our strength, He is our savior. We rest in Him with faith that He will guide us through even the toughest of situations. We trust that He will rescue us. This brings us true joy — the real kind that entertainment cannot equal. There is no movie, there is no game, there is no thing that can come near to the joy God brings us. When we learn to be close to God all of the time and not just when we have troubles, we will live in the presence and action of joy forever; His joy is everlasting! Don't forget, His joy is also ours! We simply need to make it ours by claiming Him. Don't wait for a problem to remind you that God is nearby; know that He is in your presence every moment of your life.

"So, I say, let the Holy Spirit guide your lives. Then you won't be doing what your sinful nature craves."

> Galatians 5:16

guiding light . . .
moonstruck, the dove
leads our way

When we are "self-driven," we are more likely to mess up as we strike out on our own than if we travel with God — God-driven. His nature, His Holy Spirit, is the very essence of himself, God's core. He shares His leadership, love, and grace through His Holy Spirit. Holy, in this reference, means to "set aside for something very, very special — for a single purpose. We recognize His holiness and set Him aside for communing, for worship. He is God; there is just one. Jesus spent his life educating people that there is one God — not many, not thousands, but one. Jesus taught that we should be thankful for Him, that we should be thankful for His mindfulness and for His altruistic desire to please us. God served us first! Now, it's our place to serve Him. While we might crave, we must not surrender to anything but God, Himself. Our sinful desire can be unacceptably powerful. In His presence, though, sin will fade and lose its influence. Therefore, our tactic should be to keep God present at all times, without exception. If we remain in constant contact with Him, we will lead a more loving, sinless life. We are told to "remain in prayer with God at all times." This an idiom meaning that we should continuously have

Him on our minds, in our decisions, and on our hearts — without wavering. Jeremiah says, "You will seek me and find me when you seek me with all your heart," ~ (*Jeremiah 29:13*). Lead a heart-driven life where the Holy Spirit, God's very nature is your only guiding light.

Let's Pray

Search my heart, Lord and cleanse me of the slime of self-centeredness that I may live without seeing or treating you like a commodity. You do not owe me anything but you provide for all that I need simply because you love me immensely. I choose to turn away from nudging you to adapt to my will and then act rebelliously or feel hurt when it does not happen. I take charge of my heart and incline it in your direction for I trust that your wisdom will always be greater than mine. Consume me, Father until I am no longer divided, being a certain way when communing with you and being different in the presence of everyone else. Teach me how to incorporate the rest of my life into my prayer life instead of trying to edit in small conversations with you here and there. You are not meant to adjust to my schedule; you deserve more of me than I have ever offered. So, Father, I renew my relationship with you and I ask that your Divine Spirit returns to me in every area of my life.

In Jesus' name, I pray.

**"Because of your unfailing love, I can enter your house;
I will worship at your Temple with deepest awe.**
⁸ Lead me in the right path, O Lord,
or my enemies will conquer me.
Make your way plain for me to follow.
⁹ My enemies cannot speak a truthful word.
Their deepest desire is to destroy others.
Their talk is foul, like the stench from an open grave.
Their tongues are filled with flattery.[a]
¹⁰ O God, declare them guilty.
Let them be caught in their own traps.
Drive them away because of their many sins,
for they have rebelled against you.
¹¹ **But let all who take refuge in you rejoice;
let them sing joyful praises forever.
Spread your protection over them,
that all who love your name may be filled with joy."**

Psalm 5:7-11

*temple bell —
your call awakens me
just in time*

Yes! We sin! We turn from God. But God's love for us is limitless. He keeps His temple open to us without regard to our actions. His "unfailing love" prevails — even against our choices to sin. We are made imperfect; we are made "slightly less than." God has given us free will, free choice; why would He damn us for using it? We are imperfect. Imperfection cannot and will not ever be perfect. and will not ever be perfect. It's the nature of it. God, through His limitless love, knows this — He is our Creator! It isn't wise nor fair to take advantage of His love, but it is more ridiculous to ignore it!

He loves us no matter what. He is our Father and He is the very essence of perfect love. "We can love because He first loved us," ~ (1 John 4:19). God gives us "grace upon grace," (John 1:16). It is on us though, to repent — to turn back to our Father. Having a relationship with Him is on us — He is ready. Become ready, too.

"The Lord replies, "I have seen violence done to the helpless,
and I have heard the groans of the poor.
Now I will rise up to rescue them,
as they have longed for me to do."
⁶ The Lord's promises are pure,
like silver refined in a furnace,
purified seven times over.
⁷ Therefore, Lord, we know you will protect the oppressed,
preserving them forever from this lying generation,
⁸ even though the wicked strut about,
and evil is praised throughout the land."

Psalm 12:5-8

*rolling grass —
a shepherd sings,
"Glory to God!"*

Sing praise to the Lord. His promises are pure; His love is perfect. Reach to the sky and offer Him everything you have. Do this in thanks for Him gifting it to you. Your talents, when pursued, speak cosmic volumes about how God works in your life. He loves you; He created you intentionally: He gifted you a thousand abilities. Explore yourself, discover God's counsel. Feel His presence within you, anointing your way. Go into the field. Sing praise to God. Regardless of how unimportant or important you are on this earth; you are everything to God. There is no lesser nor greater in His eyes; there are only those who choose to follow Him or deny Him. "Sing glory to God for His unwavering protection, love, and grace."

"Wisdom will save you from evil people, from those whose words are twisted."

>Proverbs 2:12

silence not broken an owl glides his freedom

Wisdom of when to speak; wisdom of when not to. Wisdom of what to say; wisdom on what to hold back. Insight leads to safety. Reservation holds one back from making mistakes. Evil is evil and it beckons in unlimited ways. Evil speaks the languages of lies, arrogance, ignorance — all languages of damage and not one of good. Evil can pretend to be good, but isn't. Most of all evil reveals itself through its actions to cause unrest, hurt, and hate; other qualities that defines itself are its judgement, pettiness, lack of responsibility, blaming others for its choices, turning people against people — the list is long. Wisdom is the antidote to evil. The quickest way to defeat evil is through wisdom. Wisdom's source is God. Evil is conquered by God. Ask for wisdom when you pray. The more you connect to wisdom, the less you are bound by evil. Evil has no chains strong enough to restrain God. Through God, evil has no chains powerful enough to restrain you!

"Understand this, my dear brothers and sisters: You must all **be quick to listen, slow to speak, and slow to get angry**."

James 1:19

words unsaid;
their fury contained
by grace

James teaches a powerful lesson in this verse. If only people would adhere to his advice today — to listen well, to speak mindfully, and to be cautious about becoming angry. Anger is always the cause of trouble, never the solution. Anger shuts down all mutual communication and is a significant stressor, not a cure — anger agitates rather than resolves dissonance. No one is happy when they are angry, even if they win the argument. Happiness — joy — both come from peace, from peaceful hearts. There is no pathway that makes anger the genesis of peace. James teaches that we should be quick to listen. He doesn't qualify it. Just listen! And do it now! Listening is the first step to understanding and resolving dissonance. Holding back your words is step two. Be slow to speak. Be mindful of what you say. "Hold your tongue." Anger and the tongue might be friends but when combined, they are weapons of war. Hold back. Speak little. Remain mindful. Listen well. And, be very, very slow to anger because much of what anger brings about between people cannot be undone.

"But you, O Lord, are a God merciful and gracious, **slow to anger** and **abounding in steadfast love and faithfulness**."

Psalm 86:15

moonrise
the deep silence
from within

"Slow to anger" is often referenced in the Bible. The Old Testament as well as the New include this admonishment. Be slow to anger — if only every last one of us would embrace this way of slowness — Jesus's Way of peace. Silence through God is always best. While there is a time for anger, it shouldn't become the norm — a recurring personality trait. It should arise only if it is righteous, as the only fair and reasonable action under the auspices of God. Anger should not become a lifestyle. These days, however, people become angry and vengeful, even jumping to reactions that are greater than the reason(s) for it. This magnitude of a response engages too much destructive power and it will destroy you as much as the target of your anger. Instead of living in anger, pray to God for peace to dwell within your heart. Pray for the target of your anger as well. And, especially, pray that you do not remain under the continuing spell of your anger. Have no doubt; anger is evil. It will destroy you and others around you. It is crucial to understand that anger will never be the soil for peace.

"If you carefully listen to the commands which I am giving you today, to love the Lord your God and to serve him with all your heart and all your soul . . ."

>Deuteronomy 11:13

lost sheep . . .
found by the light
of His call

Moses was encouraging a strong relationship between humans and God. He wanted egos to submit (become empty) so that it would be possible. Through complete surrender to God, our Father, the ability to serve not only Him but all people, arises. He wanted his tribe to be "all in" for everyone, starting with God. Afterall, God has already served humanity and continues to do so every second of the day; He never lets up — providing everything we need at all times. As He serves us, we serve Him — we humble — we commit — we follow God's advice and counsel without wavering. "Serve Him with all your heart and all your soul," is Moses' lesson to his followers. His advice stands today — for us to continuously become humbler — so much so, that we nearly disappear. It is "this meek" that inherits the earth and the kingdom of heaven. Be meek; be humble. That is the voice that God hears and desires the most.

"For even the Son of Man came not to be served but to serve, and to give his life as a ransom for many."

    Mark 10:45, Matthew 20:28, Deuteronomy 10:12

making wine . . .
Jesus serves us
his life

Jesus always sets the example; he lived by his teachings. He, the Son of God, offered to serve us in order for us to live; yes, he chose to die for us. We must make the same choice every moment of our lives — to die of ourselves to be re-formed in God. We must lose ourselves to find ourselves. Our egos must be held in bondage as our spirit is freed to join Christ on the cross and fully commit ourselves to our Father. There should be no hesitation; that accomplishes nothing. Jesus served so that we would learn how to serve. He taught us that being a lowly, humble servant is the highest status in the Kingdom of Heaven. Afterall, who can teach the arrogant? Not even God can do that.

"As each has received a gift, use it well to serve one another, as good stewards of God's grace."

1 Peter 4:10-11

offering a rose
the sunset lights
its fire

It's a stunning thought that Jesus gave his life for us; it's the most profound moment in human history. He loved us so much that he served us by serving up himself. He is resurrected in order for us to be overwhelmed in awe (humbled); he proves his Word. We are together, as a result, lit by his light; we are on fire with his Word. We are filled with the Holy Spirit as Jesus' gift. We are the spiritual DNA of God, our Father. And now, we serve the Kingdom, God's Kingdom, and we are made complete.

Let's Pray

We thank you for this beautiful day, Father. We praise you in all your greatness. We are grateful that you love us so dearly; you sent Jesus as the manifestation of your love in the flesh. When we are met at the door with disappointment, Jesus shows up as another door. He embraces us as we are — clothed in brokenness, limitations, and anguish. He strips us off of our self-sufficiency and redirects the rejection that we are faced with into higher revelation, along with the gift to experience your resurrection power. Father, bless us with the wisdom to distinguish where we need to persevere from the battles, we need to hand over to you. Lord, as we gather here today, please send the Holy Spirit upon us and open our hearts to allow Jesus to guide us through his door into your boundless love.

Jesus said, "I am the door. If anyone enters by me, he will be saved and will go in and out, and find pasture."

In Jesus' name, we pray.

"You are the light of the world."

    Matthew 5:14

new dawn
this rising light
weaves my mind

Jesus was encouraging his disciples to understand that they were to make manifest his message. Christ taught that the apostles and others were to educate and reform all people. The Jews were far from in touch with God and leading lives of carelessness, arrogance, and sin. They were miserable but didn't even know it. Their doctrine was killing them, physically and spiritually — drawing them further and further from God. The apostles learned that Jesus was the original and purest light. And it was rapidly apparent that their job was to maintain that light as his journey takes him to his stunning victory over death. Like the apostles, we need to be the continuum of the light of Christ; we must shine from a hill where all can witness our works; we must continue to deliver Christ's everlasting message that brings an absolute consciousness to everyone so they will have a chance to understand the power of Jesus' actions and message.

"Don't let anyone capture you with empty philosophies and high-sounding nonsense that come from human thinking and from the spiritual powers of this world, rather than from Christ. ⁹ For in Christ lives all the fullness of God in a human body."

    Colossians 2:8-9

oh pelican!
the sound of your voice,
your ego

There are so many people teaching what God didn't; there are so many teachers that stray from God's word as they make a living off of their own. Traps are set; the prey is us, the "we" of the earth that people attempt to attract for profit with empty teachings where Christ and his Father do not exist. We must shun all instructions that are not of God and choose to live in the fullness of God and His kingdom. Human teaching is the lesser; God's teaching is the greater. If you want your life to be greater, then follow God. He is the way; his son is the light.

"May you be filled with joy, [12] always thanking the Father. He has enabled you to share in the inheritance that belongs to his people, who live in the light."

    Colossians 1:11-12

starlight —
how grateful I am
for your guidance

Living in light is our priority. Christ died for us so that we may know God and have an eternal life with Him. Christ, who gave his life so that we may live, is our living light — the living Word of God. He brought us from darkness to the truth of God. He revealed to us an eternal kingdom. He taught us that what we do will fall away; he revealed that his teachings are the map that leads us to our forever with God, our Father.

"You can make many plans in your heart, but it is the Lord's purpose that will prevail."

Proverbs 19:21

building dens
local bears know
what's to come

The Lord's purpose, His desire is always the underlying motivation of existence, whether we accept it or not. Local bears continue to build their lives; they know and understand that what is coming is nature's winter — they must be prepared. Bears have an intrinsic knowledge of God's way; people do to. People do know, at least in the deepest sense of their being, what's to come; and yet they live in denial as their egos lead the way. Bears didn't create their habitat; they simply know how to live well within it. God did not give us a lesser understanding; He gave us "knowing." Through free will, though, we can choose to deny it; however, simply because we deny something, doesn't mean it went away somehow: truth is truth and it remains as such without regard to human opinions. I know that this sounds harsh; maybe that's the only way to reach us? Jesus' death was harsh. What else could ever wake up a collection of hardened hearts?

"For even the Son of Man came not to be served but to serve, and to give his life as a ransom for many."

Mark 10:45

grassy hills
his water delivers
everlasting life

There is only one truth, one Holy Spirit, and one God. God sent His only anointed son to serve all of humanity — as one people — without division. We wonder, from time to time, "What is our purpose?" Jesus answers that here — he came to serve, not be served. He is the example of how we should live our lives. By serving, we become complete in him and our Father, our one and only God of all creation. In many cultures (and customs), the richest are sitting back, leaning back in their chairs as they are served. Jesus, the richest in spirit, chooses not to lean back but to serve — in humbleness and love — all humanity. The greatest should serve, not the other way around. God served us; Jesus served us: and now, we wait to be served? Perhaps we should follow their lead; maybe we should become humbler and serve as well? And maybe we should do so as often as possible.

"No one can serve two masters, for either he will hate the one and love the other, or he will be devoted to the one and despise the other. You cannot serve God and money."

Matthew 6:24

> *gentle breeze . . .*
> *a mother feeds*
> *her offspring*

The admonishment is for us not to serve idols. The list of idols seems endless: money, addiction, laziness, anger, hate, statues, self. Worshipping anything but God is serving an idol; worshipping God, is the truth of serving His kingdom. It's simple: we are given food from God; we should share that food with everyone without hesitation or question. This is the choice that we all face — are we servants of God or are we servants of ourselves? Ponder for a moment; where would we be today if Jesus backed out of the deal with God? Can you imagine if he served himself instead of humanity? He made his choice; have you made yours?

"Peace Be With You"

A very special thanks to Andrea Sumadsad for offering her prayers to be included in *The Poetry of God*. She has a wonderfully sensitive relationship with God that draws from her the warmest stories and prayers that one could ever desire to hear or read. This book would not be the same without her incredible contributions.

Thank you my dear friend,

Don

www.ingramcontent.com/pod-product-compliance
Lightning Source LLC
Chambersburg PA
CBHW062217080426
42734CB00010B/1923